Love Letters of Great Men and Women:

From the Eighteenth Century

to the Present Day

Published by Megalodon Entertainment, LLC. (USA)
www.MegalodonEntertainment.com

First Printing: June 2008

Visit **MEGALODON ENTERTAINMENT LLC.** on the web at:
www.MegalodonEntertainment.com

ISBN: 1-61589-035-1
ISBN-13: 978-1-61589-035-4

BULK INQUERIES:
Quantity discounts are available on bulk orders of this novel for educational, fund-raising, promotional, and special sales purposes. For details, please contact: www.MegalodonEntertainment.com

Table of Contents

Ludwig Van Beethoven

July 6, in the morning

My angel, my all, my very self - Only a few words today and at that with pencil (with yours) - Not till tomorrow will my lodgings be definitely determined upon - what a useless waste of time - Why this deep sorrow when necessity speaks - can our love endure except through sacrifices, through not demanding everything from one another; can you change the fact that you are not wholly mine, I not wholly thine - Oh God, look out into the beauties of nature and comfort your heart with that which must be - Love demands everything and that very justly - thus it is to me with you, and to your with me. But you forget so easily that I must live for me and for you; if we were wholly united you would feel the pain of it as little as I - My journey was a fearful one; I did not reach here until 4 o'clock yesterday morning. Lacking horses the post-coach chose another route, but what an awful one; at the stage before the last I was warned not to travel at night; I was made fearful of a forest, but that only made me the more eager - and I was wrong. The coach must needs break down on the wretched road, a bottomless mud road. Without such postilions as I had with me I should have remained stuck in the road. Esterhazy, traveling the usual road here, had the same fate with eight horses that I had with four - Yet I got some pleasure out of it, as I always do when I successfully overcome difficulties - Now a quick change to things internal from things external. We shall surely see each other soon; moreover, today I cannot share with you the thoughts I have had during these last few days touching my own life - If our hearts were always close together, I would have none of these. My heart is full of so many things to say to you - ah - there are moments when I feel that speech amounts to nothing at all - Cheer up - remain my true, my only treasure, my all as I am yours. The gods must send us the rest, what for us must and shall be -

Ludwig Van Beethoven

Evening, Monday, July 6

You are suffering, my dearest creature - only now have I learned that letters must be posted very early in the morning on Mondays to Thursdays - the only days on which the mail-coach goes from here to K. - You are suffering - Ah, wherever I am, there you are also - I will arrange it with you and me that I can live with you. What a life!!! thus!!! without you - pursued by the goodness of mankind hither and thither - which I as little want to deserve as I deserve it - Humility of man towards man - it pains me - and when I consider myself in relation to the universe, what am I and what is He - whom we call the greatest - and yet - herein lies the divine in man - I weep when I reflect that you will probably not receive the first report from me until Saturday - Much as you love me - I love you more - But do not ever conceal yourself from me - good night - As I am taking the baths I must go to bed - Oh God - so near! so far! Is not our love truly a heavenly structure, and also as firm as the vault of heaven?

Ludwig Van Beethoven

Good morning, on July 7

Though still in bed, my thoughts go out to you, my Immortal Beloved, now and then joyfully, then sadly, waiting to learn whether or not fate will hear us - I can live only wholly with you or not at all - Yes, I am resolved to wander so long away from you until I can fly to your arms and say that I am really at home with you, and can send my soul enwrapped in you into the land of spirits - Yes, unhappily it must be so - You will be the more contained since you know my fidelity to you. No one else can ever possess my heart - never - never - Oh God, why must one be parted from one whom one so loves. And yet my life in V is now a wretched life - Your love makes me at once the happiest and the unhappiest of men - At my age I need a steady, quiet life - can that be so in our connection? My angel, I have just been told that the mailcoach goes every day - therefore I must close at once so that you may receive the letter at once - Be calm, only by a calm consideration of our existence can we achieve our purpose to live together - Be calm - love me - today - yesterday - what tearful longings for you - you - you - my life - my all - farewell. Oh continue to love me - never misjudge the most faithful heart of your beloved.

ever thine
ever mine
ever ours

Voltaire

The Hague 1713

I am a prisoner here in the name of the King;
they can take my life, but not the love that I feel for you.

Yes, my adorable mistress, to-night I shall see you, if I had to put
my head on the block to do it.

For heaven's sake, do not speak to me in such disastrous terms as
you write; you must live and be cautious; beware of Madame your
mother as of your worst enemy.

What do I say?

Beware of everybody; trust no one; keep yourself in readiness, as
soon as the moon is visible; I shall leave the hotel incognito, take a
carriage or a chaise, we shall drive like the wind to Sheveningen; I
shall take paper and ink with me; we shall write our letters.

If you love me, reassure yourself; and call all your strength and
presence of mind to your aid; do not let your mother notice anything,
try to have your pictures, and be assured that the menace of the
greatest tortures will not prevent me to serve you.

No, nothing has the power to part me from you; our love is based
upon virtue, and will last as long as our lives.

Adieu, there is nothing that I will not brave for your sake; you
deserve much more than that.

Adieu, my dear heart!

Arout (Voltaire)

Vincent Van Gogh

September 7, 1881

Life has become very dear to me, and I am very glad that I love. My life and my love are one. "But you are faced with a 'no, never never'" is your reply. My answer to that is, "Old boy, for the present I look upon that 'no, never never' as a block of ice which I press to my heart to thaw."

Dylan Thomas

March 16, 1950

Cat: my cat: If only you would write to me: My love, oh Cat.

This is not, as it seems from the address above, a dive, a joint, saloon, etc. but the honourable & dignified headquarters of the dons of the University of Chicago.

I love you. That is all I know. But all I know, too, is that I am writing into space: the kind of dreadful, unknown space I am just going to enter. I am going to Iowa, Illinois, Idaho, Indindiana, but these, though mis-spelt, *are* on the map. You are not.

Have you forgotten me? I am the man you used to say you loved. I used to sleep in your arms - do you remember? But you never write. You are perhaps mindless of me. I am not of you. I love you.

There isn't a moment of any hideous day when I do not say to myself. 'It will be alright. I shall go home. Caitlin loves me. I love Caitlin.' But perhaps you have forgotten. If you have forgotten, or lost your affection for me, please, my Cat, let me know. I Love You.

Dylan

Wolfgang Amadeus Mozart

October 17, 1790

...

PS

While I was writing the last page, tear after tear fell on the paper. But I must cheer up - catch! - An astonishing number of kisses are flying about - The deuce! - I see a whole crowd of them! Ha! Ha!...I have just caught three - They are delicious! - You can still answer this letter, but you must address your reply to Linz, Poste Restante - That is the safest course. As I do not yet know for certain whether I shall go to Regensburg, I can't tell you anything definite. Just write on the cover that the letter is to be kept until called for.

Adieu - Dearest, most beloved little wife - Take care of your health - and don't think of walking into town. Do write and tell me how you like our new quarters - Adieu. I kiss you millions of times.

Abigail Adams to John Adams

My Dearest Friend,

...should I draw you the picture of my heart it would be what I hope you would still love though it contained nothing new. The early possession you obtained there, and the absolute power you have obtained over it, leaves not the smallest space unoccupied.

I look back to the early days of our acquaintance and friendship as to the days of love and innocence, and, with an indescribable pleasure, I have seen near a score of years roll over our heads with an affection heightened and improved by time, nor have the dreary years of absence in the smallest degree effaced from my mind the image of the dear untitled man to whom I gave my heart.

December 23, 1782

Sullivan Ballou

July the 14th, 1861

Washington D.C.

My very dear Sarah:

The indications are very strong that we shall move in a few days -- perhaps tomorrow. Lest I should not be able to write you again, I feel impelled to write lines that may fall under your eye when I shall be no more.

Our movement may be one of a few days duration and full of pleasure -- and it may be one of severe conflict and death to me. Not my will, but thine 0 God, be done. If it is necessary that I should fall on the battlefield for my country, I am ready. I have no misgivings about, or lack of confidence in, the cause in which I am engaged, and my courage does not halt or falter. I know how strongly American Civilization now leans upon the triumph of the Government, and how great a debt we owe to those who went before us through the blood and suffering of the Revolution. And I am willing -- perfectly willing -- to lay down all my joys in this life, to help maintain this Government, and to pay that debt.

But, my dear wife, when I know that with my own joys I lay down nearly all of yours, and replace them in this life with cares and sorrows -- when, after having eaten for long years the bitter fruit of orphanage myself, I must offer it as their only sustenance to my dear little children -- is it weak or dishonorable, while the banner of my purpose floats calmly and proudly in the breeze, that my unbounded love for you, my darling wife and children, should struggle in fierce, though useless, contest with my love of country?

I cannot describe to you my feelings on this calm summer night, when two thousand men are sleeping around me, many of them enjoying the last, perhaps, before that of death -- and I, suspicious that Death is creeping behind me with his fatal dart, am communing with God, my country, and thee.

I have sought most closely and diligently, and often in my breast, for a wrong motive in thus hazarding the happiness of those I loved and I could not find one. A pure love of my country and of the principles have often advocated before the people and "the name of honor that I love more than I fear death" have called upon me, and I have obeyed.

Sarah, my love for you is deathless, it seems to bind me to you with mighty cables that nothing but Omnipotence could break; and yet my love of Country comes over me like a strong wind and bears me irresistibly on with all these chains to the battlefield.

The memories of the blissful moments I have spent with you come creeping over me, and I feel most gratified to God and to you that I have enjoyed them so long. And hard it is for me to give them up and burn to ashes the hopes of future years, when God willing, we might still have lived and loved together and seen our sons grow up to honorable manhood around us. I have, I know, but few and small claims upon Divine Providence, but something whispers to me -- perhaps it is the wafted prayer of my little Edgar -- that I shall return to my loved ones unharmed. If I do not, my dear Sarah, never forget how much I love you, and when my last breath escapes me on the battlefield, it will whisper your name.

Forgive my many faults, and the many pains I have caused you. How thoughtless and foolish I have oftentimes been! How gladly would I wash out with my tears every little spot upon your happiness, and struggle with all the misfortune of this world, to shield you and my children from harm. But I cannot. I must watch you from the spirit land and hover near you, while you buffet the storms with your precious little freight, and wait with sad patience till we meet to part no more.

But, O Sarah! If the dead can come back to this earth and flit unseen around those they loved, I shall always be near you; in the garish day and in the darkest night -- amidst your happiest scenes and gloomiest hours -- always, always; and if there be a soft breeze upon your cheek, it shall be my breath; or the cool air fans your throbbing temple, it shall be my spirit passing by.

Sarah, do not mourn me dead; think I am gone and wait for thee, for we shall meet again.

As for my little boys, they will grow as I have done, and never know a father's love and care. Little Willie is too young to remember me long, and my blue-eyed Edgar will keep my frolics with him among the dimmest memories of his childhood. Sarah, I have unlimited confidence in your maternal care and your development of their characters. Tell my two mothers his and hers I call God's blessing upon them. O Sarah, I wait for you there! Come to me, and lead thither my children.

Sullivan

Harriet Beecher Stowe

January 1, 1847

My Dearest Husband

...I was at that date of marriage a very different being from what I am now and stood in relation to my Heavenly Father in a very different attitude. My whole desire was to live in love, absorbing passionate devotion to one person. Our separation was my first trial -- but then came a note of comfort in the hope of being a mother. No creature ever so longed to see the face of a little one or had such a heart full of love to bestow. Here came in trial again sickness, pain, perplexity, constant discouragement -- wearing wasting days and nights -- a cross, deceitful, unprincipled nurse -- husband gone... When you came back you came only to increasing perplexities.

Ah, how little comfort I had in being a mother -- how was all that I proposed met and crossed and my may ever hedged up!

...In short, God would teach me that I should make no family be my chief good and portion and bitter as the lesson has been I thank Him for it from my very soul. One might naturally infer that from the union of two both morbidly sensitive and acute, yet in many respects exact opposites -- one hasty and impulsive -- the other sensitive and brooding -- one the very personification of exactness and routine and the other to whom everything of the kind was an irksome effort -- from all this what should one infer but some painful friction.

But all this would not after all have done so very much had not Providence as if intent to try us throws upon the heaviest external pressure... but still where you have failed your faults have been to me those of one beloved -- of the man who after all would be the choice of my heart still were I to choose -- for were I now free I should again love just as I did and again feel that I could give up all to and for you -- and if I do not love never can love again with the blind and unwise love with which I married I love quite as truly tho far more wisely...

In reflecting upon our future union -- our marriage -- the past obstacles to our happiness -- it seems to me that they are of two or three kinds. 1st those from physical causes both in you and in me -- such on your part as hypochondriac morbid instability for which the only remedy is physical care and attention to the laws of health -- and on my part an excess of sensitiveness and of confusion and want of control of mind and memory. This always increases on my part in proportion as a I blamed and found fault with and I hope will decrease with returning health. I hope that we shall both be impressed with a most solemn sense of the importance of a wise and constant attention to the laws of health.

Then in the second place the want of any definite plan of mutual watchfulness, with regard to each other's improvement, of a definite time and place for doing it with a firm determination to improve and be improved by each other -- to confess our faults one to another and pray one for another that we may be healed...

Yours with much love

H.

Pietro Bembo

Venice October 18, 1503

Eight days have passed since I parted from f.f., and already it is as though I had been eight years away from her, although I can avow that not one hour has passed without her memory which has become such a close companion to my thoughts that now more than ever is it the food and sustenance of my soul; and if it should endure like this a few days more, as seems it must, I truly believe it will in every way have assumed the office of my soul, and I shall then live and thrive on the memory of her as do other men upon their souls, and I shall have no life but in this single thought.

Let the God who so decrees do as he will, so long as in exchange I may have as much a part of her as shall suffice to prove the gospel of our affinity is founded on true prophecy. Often I find myself recalling, and with what ease, certain words spoken to me, some on the balcony with the moon as witness, others at that window I shall always look upon so gladly, with all the many endearing and gracious acts I have seen my gentle lady perform--for all are dancing about my heart with a tenderness so wondrous that they inflame me with a strong desire to beg her to test the quality of my love.

For I shall never rest content until I am certain she knows what she is able to enact in me and how great and strong is the fire that her great worth has kindled in my breast. The flame of true love is a mighty force, and most of all when two equally matched wills in two exalted minds contend to see which loves the most, each striving to give yet more vital proof...

It would be the greatest delight for me to see just two lines in f.f.'s hand, yet I dare not ask so much. May your Ladyship beseech her to perform whatever you feel is best for me. With my heart I kiss your Ladyship's hand, since I cannot with my lips.

Napoleon Bonaparte

Paris, December 1795

I wake filled with thoughts of you. Your portrait and the intoxicating evening which we spent yesterday have left my senses in turmoil. Sweet, incomparable Josephine, what a strange effect you have on my heart! Are you angry? Do I see you looking sad? Are you worried?... My soul aches with sorrow, and there can be no rest for you lover; but is there still more in store for me when, yielding to the profound feelings which overwhelm me, I draw from your lips, from your heart a love which consumes me with fire? Ah! it was last night that I fully realized how false an image of you your portrait gives!

You are leaving at noon; I shall see you in three hours.

Until then, mio dolce amor, a thousand kisses; but give me none in return, for they set my blood on fire.

Napoleon Bonaparte

Spring 1797

To Josephine,

I love you no longer; on the contrary, I detest you. you are a wretch, truly perverse, truly stupid, a real Cinderella. You never write to me at all, you do not love your husband; you know the pleasure that your letters give him yet you cannot even manage to write him half a dozen lines, dashed off in a moment! What then do you do all day, Madame? What business is so vital that it robs you of the time to write to your faithful lover? What attachment can be stifling and pushing aside the love, the tender and constant love which you promised him? Who can this wonderful new lover be who takes up your every moment, rules your days and prevents you from devoting your attention to your husband?

Beware, Josephine; one fine night the doors will be broken down and there I shall be. In truth, I am worried, my love, to have no news from you; write me a four page letter instantly made up from those delightful words which fill my heart with emotion and joy. I hope to hold you in my arms before long, when I shall lavish upon you a million kisses, burning as the equatorial sun.

Charlotte Bronte

January 8, 1845

Monsieur, the poor have not need of much to sustain them -- they ask only for the crumbs that fall from the rich man's table. But if they are refused the crumbs they die of hunger. Nor do I, either, need much affection from those I love. I should not know what to do with a friendship entire and complete - I am not used to it. But you showed me of yore a little interest, when I was your pupil in Brussels, and I hold on to the maintenance of that little interest -- I hold on to it as I would hold on to life.

Rupert Brooke

October 2, 1911

I have a thousand images of you in an hour; all different and all coming back to the same... And we love. And we've got the most amazing secrets and understandings. Noel, whom I love, who is so beautiful and wonderful. I think of you eating omlette on the ground. I think of you once against a sky line: and on the hill that Sunday morning.

And that night was wonderfullest of all. The light and the shadow and quietness and the rain and the wood. And you. You are so beautiful and wonderful that I daren't write to you... And kinder than God.
Your arms and lips and hair and shoulders and voice - you.

Rupert Brooke

Elizabeth Barrett Browning

To Robert Browning:

And now listen to me in turn. You have touched me more profoundly than I thought even you could have touched me - my heart was full when you came here today. Henceforward I am yours for everything....

- Elizabeth Barrett Browning

(1806-1861)

Robert Browning

To Elizabeth Barrett Browning:

...would I, if I could, supplant one of any of the affections that I know to have taken root in you - that great and solemn one, for instance. I feel that if I could get myself remade, as if turned to gold, I WOULD not even then desire to become more than the mere setting to that diamond you must always wear.

The regard and esteem you now give me, in this letter, and which I press to my heart and bow my head upon, is all I can take and all too embarrassing, using all my gratitude.

- Robert Browning

(1812-1889)

Robert Browning

January 10, 1846

Do you know, when you have told me to think of you, I have been feeling ashamed of thinking of you so much, of thinking of only you--which is too much, perhaps. Shall I tell you? It seems to me, to myself, that no man was ever before to any woman what you are to me--the fullness must be in proportion, you know, to the vacancy...and only I know what was behind--the long wilderness without the blossoming rose...and the capacity for happiness, like a black gaping hole, before this silver flooding. Is it wonderful that I should stand as in a dream, and disbelieve--not you--but my own fate?

Was ever any one taken suddenly from a lampless dungeon and placed upon the pinnacle of a mountain, without the head turning round and the heart turning faint, as mine do? And you love me more, you say?--Shall I thank you or God? Both,--indeed--and there is no possible return from me to either of you! I thank you as the unworthy may.. and as we all thank God. How shall I ever prove what my heart is to you? How will you ever see it as I feel it? I ask myself in vain. Have so much faith in me, my only beloved, as to use me simply for your own advantage and happiness, and to your own ends without a thought of any others--that is all I could ask you without any disquiet as to the granting of it--May God bless you! --Your B.A.

Robert Burdette

April 25, 1898

And when I have reasoned it all out, and set metes and bounds for your love that it may not pass, lo, a letter from Clara, and in one sweet, ardent, pure, Edenic page, her love overrides my boudaries as the sea sweeps over rocks and sands alike, crushes my barriers into dust out of which they were builded, over whelms me with its beauty, bewilders me with its sweetness, charms me with its purity, and loses me in its great shoreless immensity.

George Bernard Shaw

18th November 1912

33 Kensington Square

No more shams -- a real love letter this time -- then I can breathe freely, and perhaps who knows begin to sit up and get well –

I haven't said 'kiss me' because life is too short for the kiss my heart calls for... All your words are as idle wind -- Look into my eyes for two minutes without speaking if you dare! Where would be your 54 years? and my grandmother's heart? and how many hours would you be late for dinner?

-- If you give me one kiss and you can only kiss me if I say 'kiss me' and I will never say 'kiss me' because I am a respectable widow and I wouldn't let any man kiss me unless I was sure of the wedding ring –

Stella
(Liza, I mean).

Lord Byron

August 1812

My dearest Caroline,

If tears, which you saw & know I am not apt to shed, if the agitation in which I parted from you, agitation which you must have perceived through the whole of this most nervous nervous affair, did not commence till the moment of leaving you approached, if all that I have said & done, & am still but too ready to say & do, have not sufficiently proved what my real feelings are & must be ever towards you, my love, I have no other proof to offer.

God knows I wish you happy, & when I quit you, or rather when you from a sense of duty to your husband & mother quit me, you shall acknowledge the truth of what I again promise & vow, that no other in word or deed shall ever hold the place in my affection which is & shall be most sacred to you, till I am nothing.

I never knew till that moment, the madness of -- my dearest & most beloved friend -- I cannot express myself -- this is no time for words -- but I shall have a pride, a melancholy pleasure, in suffering what you yourself can hardly conceive -- for you don not know me. -- I am now about to go out with a heavy heart, because -- my appearing this Evening will stop any absurd story which the events of today might give rise to -- do you think now that I am cold & stern, & artful -- will even others think so, will your mother even -- that mother to whom we must indeed sacrifice much, more much more on my part, than she shall ever know or can imagine.

"Promises not to love you" ah Caroline it is past promising -- but shall attribute all concessions to the proper motive -- & never cease to feel all that you have already witnessed -- & more than can ever be known but to my own heart -- perhaps to yours -- May God protect forgive & bless you -- ever & even more than ever.

yr. most attached

BYRON

P.S. -- These taunts which have driven you to this -- my dearest Caroline -- were it not for your mother & the kindness of all your connections, is there anything on earth or heaven would have made me so happy as to have made you mine long ago? & not less now than then, but more than ever at this time -- you know I would with pleasure give up all here & all beyond the grave for you -- & in refraining from this -- must my motives be misunderstood --? I care not who knows this -- what use is made of it -- it is you & to you only that they owe yourself, I was and am yours, freely & most entirely, to obey, to honour, love --& fly with you when, where, & how you yourself might & may determine.

Lord Byron

November 16, 1814

My Heart –

We are thus far separated - but after all one mile is as bad as a thousand - which is a great consolation to one who must travel six hundred before he meets you again. If it will give you any satisfaction - I am as comfortless as a pilgrim with peas in his shoes - and as cold as Charity - Chastity or any other Virtue.

Lord Byron

25 August, 1819

My dearest Teresa,

I have read this book in your garden;--my love, you were absent, or else I could not have read it. It is a favourite book of yours, and the writer was a friend of mine. You will not understand these English words, and others will not understand them,--which is the reason I have not scrawled them in Italian. But you will recognize the handwriting of him who passionately loved you, and you will divine that, over a book which was yours, he could only think of love.

In that word, beautiful in all languages, but most so in yours--Amor mio--is comprised my existence here and hereafter. I feel I exist here, and I feel I shall exist hereafter,--to what purpose you will decide; my destiny rests with you, and you are a woman, eighteen years of age, and two out of a convent. I love you, and you love me,--at least, you say so, and act as if you did so, which last is a great consolation in all events.

But I more than love you, and cannot cease to love you. Think of me, sometimes, when the Alps and ocean divide us, --but they never will, unless you wish it.

Lewis Carroll

Christ Church, Oxford, October 28, 1876

My Dearest Gertrude:

You will be sorry, and surprised, and puzzled, to hear what a queer illness I have had ever since you went. I sent for the doctor, and said, "Give me some medicine. for I'm tired." He said, "Nonsense and stuff! You don't want medicine: go to bed!"

I said, "No; it isn't the sort of tiredness that wants bed. I'm tired in the face." He looked a little grave, and said, "Oh, it's your nose that's tired: a person often talks too much when he thinks he knows a great deal." I said, "No, it isn't the nose. Perhaps it's the hair." Then he looked rather grave, and said, "Now I understand: you've been playing too many hairs on the pianoforte."

"No, indeed I haven't!" I said, "and it isn't exactly the hair: it's more about the nose and chin." Then he looked a good deal graver, and said, "Have you been walking much on your chin lately?" I said, "No." "Well!" he said, "it puzzles me very much.

Do you think it's in the lips?" "Of course!" I said. "That's exactly what it is!"

Then he looked very grave indeed, and said, "I think you must have been giving too many kisses." "Well," I said, "I did give one kiss to a baby child, a little friend of mine."

"Think again," he said; "are you sure it was only one?" I thought again, and said, "Perhaps it was eleven times." Then the doctor said, "You must not give her any more till your lips are quite rested again." "But what am I to do?" I said, "because you see, I owe her a hundred and eighty-two more." Then he looked so grave that tears ran down his cheeks, and he said, "You may send them to her in a box."

Then I remembered a little box that I once bought at Dover, and thought I would someday give it to some little girl or other. So I have packed them all in it very carefully. Tell me if they come safe or if any are lost on the way."

Lewis Carroll

Catherine of Aragon

1535

My Lord and Dear Husband,

I commend me unto you. The hour of my death draweth fast on, and my case being such, the tender love I owe you forceth me, with a few words, to put you in remembrance of the health and safeguard of your soul, which you ought to prefer before all worldly matters, and before the care and tendering of your own body, for the which you have cast me into many miseries and yourself into many cares.

For my part I do pardon you all, yea, I do wish and devoutly pray God that He will also pardon you.

For the rest I commend unto you Mary, our daughter, beseeching you to be a good father unto her, as I heretofore desired. I entreat you also, on behalf of my maids, to give them marriage-portions, which is not much, they being but three. For all my other servants, I solicit a year's pay more than their due, lest they should be unprovided for.

Lastly, do I vow, that mine eyes desire you above all things.

Randolf Churchill

August 1873

I cannot keep myself from writing any longer to you dearest, although I have not had any answer to either of my two letters. I suppose your mother does not allow you to write to me. Perhaps you have not got either of my letters...I am so dreadfully afraid that perhaps you may think I am forgetting you.

I can assure you dearest Jeannette you have not been out of my thoughts hardly for one minute since I left you Monday. I have written to my father everything, how much I love you how much I long & pray & how much I would sacrifice if it were necessary to be married to you and to live ever after with you.

I shall [not] get an answer till Monday & whichever way it lies I shall go to Cowes soon after & tell your mother everything. I am afraid she does not like me very much from what I have heard...I would do anything she wished if she only would not oppose us. Dearest if you are as fond of me as I am of you...nothing human could keep us long apart.

This last week has seemed an eternity to me; Oh, I would give my soul for another of those days we had together not long ago...Oh if I could only get one line from you to reassure me, but I dare not ask you to do anything that your mother would disapprove of or has perhaps forbidden you to do... Sometimes I doubt so I cannot help it whether you really like me as you said at Cowes you did. If you do I cannot fear for the future tho' difficulties may lie in our way only to be surmounted by patience.

Goodbye dearest Jeannette. My first and only love...Believe me ever to be Yrs devotedly and lovingly,

Randolf S. Churchill

Winston Churchill

January 23, 1935

My darling Clemmie,

In your letter from Madras you wrote some words very dear to me, about my having enriched your life. I cannot tell you what pleasure this gave me, because I always feel so overwhelmingly in your debt, if there can be accounts in love.... What it has been to me to live all these years in your heart and companionship no phrases can convey.

Time passes swiftly, but is it not joyous to see how great and growing is the treasure we have gathered together, amid the storms and stresses of so many eventful and to millions tragic and terrible years?

Your loving husband

(Winston Churchill)

Jane Clairmont to Lord Byron

You bid me write short to you and I have much to say. You also bade me believe that it was a fancy which made me cherish an attachment for you. It cannot be a fancy since you have been for the last year the object upon which every solitary moment led me to muse.

I do not expect you to love me, I am not worthy of your love. I feel you are superior, yet much to my surprise, more to my happiness, you betrayed passions I had believed no longer alive in your bosom. Shall I also have to ruefully experience the want of happiness? Shall I reject it when it is offered? I may appear to you imprudent, vicious; my opinions detestable, my theory depraved; but one thing, at least, time shall show you: that I love gently and with affection, that I am incapable of anything approaching to the feeling of revenge or malice; I do assure you, your future will shall be mine, and everything you shall do or say, I shall not question.

1815

Samuel Langhorne Clemens (Mark Twain)

May 12, 1869

Out of the depths of my happy heart wells a great tide of love and prayer for this priceless treasure that is confided to my life-long keeping.

You cannot see its intangible waves as they flow towards you, darling, but in these lines you will hear, as it were, the distant beating of the surf.

John Constable

East Bergholt. February 27, 1816

I received your letter my ever dearest Maria, this morning. You know my anxious disposition too well not be aware how much I feel at this time. At the distance we are from each other every fear will obtrude itself on my mind. Let me hope that you are not really worse than your kindness, your affection, for me make you say...I think...that no more molestation will arise to the recovery of your health, which I pray for beyond every other blessing under heaven.

Let us...think only of the blessings that providence may yet have in store for us and that we may yet possess. I am happy in love--an affection exceeding a thousand times my deserts, which has continued so many years, and is yet undiminished...Never will I marry in this world if I marry not you. Truly can I say that for the seven years since I avowed my love for you, I have...foregone all company, and the society of all females (except my own relations) for your sake.

I am still ready to make my sacrifice for you...I will submit to any thing you may command me--but cease to respect, to love and adore you I never can or will. I must still think that we should have married long ago--we should have had many troubles--but we have yet had no joys, and we could not have starved...Your FRIENDS have never been without a hope of parting us and see what that has cost us both--but no more.

Believe me, my beloved & ever dearest Maria, most faithfully yours,

John

Duff Cooper

June 9, 1914

Don't write too legibly or intelligibly as I have no occupation so pleasant as pondering for hours over your hieroglyphics, and for hours more trying to interpret your dark sayings. A clearly written simply expressed letter is too like the lightening.

Duff Cooper

August 20, 1918

Darling, my darling. One line in haste to tell you that I love you more today than ever in my life before, that I never see beauty without thinking of you or scent happiness without thinking of you. You have fulfilled all my ambition, realized all my hopes, made all my dreams come true.

You have set a crown of roses on my youth and fortified me against the disaster of our days. Your courageous gaiety has inspired me with joy. Your tender faithfulness has been a rock of security and comfort. I have felt for you all kinds of love at once.

I have asked much of you and you have never failed me. You have intensified all colours, heightened all beauty, deepened all delight. I love you more than life, my beauty, my wonder.

Oliver Cromwell

Dunbar, 4 September, 1650

For my beloved Wife Elizabeth Cromwell, at the Cockpit:

My Dearest,

I have not leisure to write much, but I could chide thee that in many of thy letters thou writest to me, that I should not be unmindful of thee and thy little ones. Truly, if I love thee not too well, I think I err not on the other hand much. Thou art dearer to me than any creature; let that suffice.

The Lord hath showed us an exceeding mercy: who can tell how great it is. My weak faith hath been upheld. I have been in my inward man marvellously supported; though I assure thee, I grow an old man, and feel infirmities of age marvellously stealing upon me. Would my corruptions did as fast decrease. Pray on my behalf in the latter respect. The particulars of our late success Harry Vane or Gil. Pickering will impart to thee. My love to all dear friends. I rest thine,

Oliver Cromwell

Pierre Curie

August 10, 1894

Nothing could have given me greater pleasure that to get news of you. The prospect of remaining two months without hearing about you had been extremely disagreeable to me: that is to say, your little note was more than welcome.

I hope you are laying up a stock of good air and that you will come back to us in October. As for me, I think I shall not go anywhere; I shall stay in the country, where I spend the whole day in front of my open window or in the garden.

We have promised each other -- haven't we? -- to be at least great friends. If you will only not change your mind! For there are no promises that are binding; such things cannot be ordered at will. It would be a fine thing, just the same, in which I hardly dare believe, to pass our lives near each other, hypnotized by our dreams: your patriotic dream, our humanitarian dream, and our scientific dream.

Of all those dreams the last is, I believe, the only legitimate one. I mean by that that we are powerless to change the social order and, even if we were not, we should not know what to do; in taking action, no matter in what direction, we should never be sure of not doing more harm than good, by retarding some inevitable evolution. From the scientific point of view, on the contrary, we may hope to do something; the ground is solider here, and any discovery that we may make, however small, will remain acquired knowledge.

See how it works out: it is agreed that we shall be great friends, but if you leave France in a year it would be an altogether too Platonic friendship, that of two creatures who would never see each other again. Wouldn't it be better for you to stay with me? I know that this question angers you, and that you don't want to speak of it again --

and then, too, I feel so thoroughly unworthy of you from every point of view.

I thought of asking your permission to meet you by chance in Fribourg. But you are staying there, unless I am mistaken, only one day, and on that day you will of course belong to our friends the Kovalskis.

Believe me your very devoted

Peirre Curie

Alfred de Musset

September 1, 1834

But let me have this letter, containing nothing but your love; and tell me that you give me your lips, your hair, all that face that I have possessed, and tell me that we embrace - you and I!

O God, O God, when I think of it, my throat closes, my sight is troubled; my knees fail, ah, it is horrible to die, it is also horrible to love like this! What longing, what longing I have for you! I beg you to let me have the letter I ask. I am dying. Farewell.

Ninon de l'Enclos

Date Unknown

Yes, Marquis, I will keep my word with you, and upon all occasions shall speak the truth, though I sometimes tell it at my own expense. I have more firmness of mind than perhaps you may imagine, and 'tis very probable that in the course of this correspondence, you will think I push this quality too far, even to severity. But then, please to remember that I have only the outside of a woman, and that my heart and mind are wholly masculine....

Shall I tell you what makes love so dangerous? 'Tis the too high idea we are apt to form it. But to speak the truth, love, considered as passion, is merely a blind instinct, that we should rate accordingly. It is an appetite, which inclines us to one object, rather than another, without our being able to account for our taste. Considered as a bond of friendship, where reason presides, it is no longer a passion and loses the very name of love. It becomes esteem: which is indeed a very pleasing appetite, but too tranquil; and therefore incapable of rousing you from you present supineness.

If you madly trace the footsteps of our ancient heroes of romance, adopting their extravagant sentiments, you will soon experience, that such false chivalry metamorphoses this charming passion into a melancholy folly; nay, often a tragical one: a perfect frenzy! but divest it of all the borrowed pomp and opinion, and you will then perceive how much it will contribute both to your happiness and pleasure. Be assured that if either reason or knight errantry should be permitted to form the union of our hearts, love would become a state of apathy and madness.

The only way to avoid these extremes, is to pursue the course I pointed out to you. At present you have no occasion for any thing more than mere amusement, and believe me, you will not meet it except among women of the character I speak of. Your heart wants occupation; and they are framed to supply the void. At least, give my prescription a fair trial, and I will be answerable for the success.

I promised to reason with you, and I think I have kept my word. Farewell...

Tomorrow the Abbé Chateauneuf, and perhaps Molière are to be with me. We are to read over the Tartuffe together, in order to make some necessary alterations. Depend upon it, Marquis, that whoever denies the maxims I have here laid down, partakes a little of that character in his play.

Honore de Balzac

Sunday 19th

My beloved angel,

I am nearly mad about you, as much as one can be mad: I cannot bring together two ideas that you do not interpose yourself between them.

I can no longer think of anything but you. In spite of myself, my imagination carries me to you. I grasp you, I kiss you, I caress you, a thousand of the most amorous caresses take possession of me.

As for my heart, there you will always be - very much so. I have a delicious sense of you there. But my God, what is to become of me, if you have deprived me of my reason? This is a monomania which, this morning, terrifies me.

I rise up every moment saying to myself, "Come, I am going there!" Then I sit down again, moved by the sense of my obligations. There is a frightful conflict. This is not life. I have never before been like that. You have devoured everything.

I feel foolish and happy as soon as I think of you. I whirl round in a delicious dream in which in one instant I live a thousand years. What a horrible situation!

Overcome with love, feeling love in every pore, living only for love, and seeing oneself consumed by griefs, and caught in a thousand spiders' threads.

O, my darling Eva, you did not know it. I picked up your card. It is there before me, and I talk to you as if you were there. I see you, as I did yesterday, beautiful, astonishingly beautiful.

Yesterday, during the whole evening, I said to myself "she is mine!" Ah! The angels are not as happy in Paradise as I was yesterday!

Honore de Balzac

October 6, 1833

Our love will bloom always fairer, fresher, more gracious, because it is a true love, and because genuine love is ever increasing.

It is a beautiful plant growing from year to year in the heart, ever extending its palms and branches, doubling every season its glorious clusters and perfumes; and, my dear life, tell me, repeat to me always, that nothing will bruise its bark or its delicate leaves, that it will grow larger in both our hearts, loved, free, watched over, like a life within our life...

Juliette Drouet to Victor Hugo

Friday 8 p.m.

If only I were a clever woman, I could describe to you my gorgeous bird, how you unite in yourself the beauties of form, plumage, and song!

I would tell you that you are the greatest marvel of all ages, and I should only be speaking the simple truth. But to put all this into suitable words, my superb one, I should require a voice far more harmonious than that which is bestowed upon my species - for I am the humble owl that you mocked at only lately, therefore, it cannot be.

I will not tell you to what degree you are dazzling and to the birds of sweet song who, as you know, are none the less beautiful and appreciative.

I am content to delegate to them the duty of watching, listening and admiring, while to myself I reserve the right of loving; this may be less attractive to the ear, but it is sweeter far to the heart.

I love you, I love you. my Victor; I can not reiterate it too often; I can never express it as much as I feel it.

I recognise you in all the beauty that surrounds me in form, in colour, in perfume, in harmonious sound: all of these mean you to me. You are superior to all. I see and admire - you are all!

You are not only the solar spectrum with the seven luminous colours, but the sun himself, that illumines, warms, and revivifies! This is what you are, and I am the lowly woman that adores you.

Juliette

Madame Dubarry

To Monsieur Duval

My dear Friend,

Yes, I have told you, and repeat it: I love you dearly.
You certainly said the same thing to me, I begin to know the world.

I will tell you what I suggest, now: pay attention. I don't want to remain a shopgirl, but a little more my own mistress, and would therefore like to find someone to keep me.

If I did not love you, I would try to get money from you; I would say to you, you shall begin by renting me a room and furnishing it; only as you told me that you are not rich, you can take me to your own place.

It will not cost you anymore rent, nor more for your table and the rest of your housekeeping. To keep me and my headdress will be the only expense, and for those give me one hundred livres a month, and that will include everything.

Thus we could both live happily, and you would never again have to complain about my refusal. If you love me, accept this proposal; but if you do not love me, then let each of us try his luck elsewhere.

Good-by, I embrace you heartily,
Jeanne Rancon (1761)

Gaius Plinius Caecilius Secundus

Circa A.D. 100

You say that you are feeling my absence very much, and your only comfort when I am not there is to hold my writings in your hand and often put them in my place by your side. I like to think that you miss me and find relief in this sort of consolation. I, too, am always reading your letters, and returning to them again and again as if they were new to me -- but this only fans the fire of my longing for you. If your letters are so dear to me, you can imagine how I delight in your company; do write as often as you can, although you give me pleasure mingled with pain.

F. Scott Fitzgerald

Spring 1919

Sweetheart,

Please, please don't be so depressed -- We'll be married soon, and then these lonesome nights will be over forever -- and until we are, I am loving, loving every tiny minute of the day and night -- Maybe you won't understand this, but sometimes when I miss you most, it's hardest to write -- and you always know when I make myself -- Just the ache of it all -- and I can't tell you. If we were together, you'd feel how strong it is -- you're so sweet when you're melancholy. I love your sad tenderness -- when I've hurt you -- That's one of the reasons I could never be sorry for our quarrels -- and they bothered you so -- Those dear, dear little fusses, when I always tried so hard to make you kiss and forget –

Scott -- there's nothing in all the world I want but you -- and your precious love -- All the material things are nothing. I'd just hate to live a sordid, colorless existence -- because you'd soon love me less -- and less -- and I'd do anything -- anything -- to keep your heart for my own -- I don't want to live -- I want to love first, and live incidentally -- Why don't you feel that I'm waiting -- I'll come to you, Lover, when you're ready -- Don't don't ever think of the things you can't give me -- You've trusted me with the dearest heart of all -- and it's so damn much more than anybody else in all the world has ever had –

How can you think deliberately of life without me -- If you should die -- O Darling -- darling Scott -- It'd be like going blind. I know I would, too, -- I'd have no purpose in life -- just a pretty -- decoration. Don't you think I was made for you? I feel like you had me ordered -- and I was delivered to you -- to be worn -- I want you to wear me, like a watch -- charm or a button hole bouquet -- to the world. And then, when we're alone, I want to help -- to know that you can't do anything without me.

I'm glad you wrote Mamma. It was such a nice sincere letter -- and mine to St. Paul was very evasive and rambling. I've never, in all my life, been able to say anything to people older than me -- Somehow I just instinctively avoid personal things with them -- even my family. Kids are so much nicer.

Isadora Duncan

Christmas Day 1904
Grand Hotel D'Europe
St. Petersbourg
Rue Michel

Just arrived this morning -- Christmas morning
Here it's the 12 of December (remember the 12 days of Christmas)

My Darling –

I don't like it at all. All the Chairs are staring at me in the most frightful way -- And there is a Lady on the Mantel piece who has taken a Great objection to me -- and I'm awfully scared –

This is no place for a person with a nice cheerful disposition like me -- it looks like those parlors in the Novels where they plot things –

All night long the train has not been flying over but going pim de pim over Great fields of snow -- vast plains of snow -- Great bare Countries covered with snow (Walt Whitman could have written 'em up fine) and over all this the Moon shining -- and across the window always a Golden shower of sparks -- from the locomotive -- it was quite worth seeing and I lay there looking out on it all and thinking of you -- of you, you dearest sweetest best darling –

The City is covered in snow and little sleighs rushing madly about -- All things go in sliders of course. I send you many little missives along the way -- Hope they arrived! –

I must go now and wash the soot off and have my Breakfast.

Give my love to Dear Dear No. 11 and to that musty little dear Home No. 6 and for your dear self my heart is overflowing with just the most unoriginal old fashionest sort of love.

Write to me -- and tell me -- I go now to splash

Your Isadora

Gustave Flaubert

August 15, 1846

I will cover you with love when next I see you, with caresses, with ecstasy. I want to gorge you with all the joys of the flesh, so that you faint and die. I want you to be amazed by me, and to confess to yourself that you had never even dreamed of such transports... When you are old, I want you to recall those few hours, I want your dry bones to quiver with joy when you think of them.

Gustave Flaubert

August 21, 1853

Have you really not noticed, then, that here of all places, in this private, personal solitude that surrounds me, I have turned to you? All the memories of my youth speak to me as I walk, just as the sea shells crunch under my feet on the beach. The crash of every wave awakens far-distant reverberations within me.

I hear the rumble of bygone days, and in my mind the whole endless series of old passions surges forward like the billows. I remember my spasms, my sorrows, gusts of desire that whistled like wind in the rigging, and vast vague longings that swirled in the dark like a flock of wild gulls in a storm cloud.

On whom should I lean, if not on you? My weary mind turns for refreshment to the thought of you as a dusty traveler might sink onto a soft and grassy bank.

Letter to Nathaniel Hawthorne

December 31, 1839

Best Beloved,

I send you some allumettes (lampshades) wherewith to kindle the taper. There are very few but my second finger could no longer perform extra duty. These will serve till the wounded one be healed, however. How beautiful is it to provide even this slightest convenience for you, dearest! I cannot tell you how much I love you, in this back-handed style. My love is not in this attitude,-- it rather bends forward to meet you.

What a year has been to us! My definition of Beauty is, that it is love, and therefore includes both truth and good. But those only who love as we do can feel the significance and force of this.

My ideas will not flow in these crooked strokes. God be with you. I am very well, and have walked far in Danvers this cold morning. I am full of the glory of the day. God bless you this night of the old year. It has proved the year of our nativity. Ha not the old earth passed away from us?--are not all things new?

Your Sophie

Nathaniel Hawthorne

5 December, 1839

Dearest,

I wish I had the gift of making rhymes, for methinks there is poetry in my head and heart since I have been in love with you. You are a Poem. Of what sort, then? Epic? Mercy on me, no! A sonnet? No; for that is too labored and artificial. You are a sort of sweet, simple, gay, pathetic ballad, which Nature is singing, sometimes with tears, sometimes with smiles, and sometimes with intermingled smiles and tears.

Johann Wolfgang von Goethe

June 17, 1784

My letters will have shown you how lovely I am. I don't dine at Court, I see few people, and take my walks alone, and at every beautiful spot I wish you were there.

I can't help loving you more than is good for me; I shall feel all the happier when I see you again. I am always conscious of my nearness to you, your presence never leaves me. In you I have a measure for every woman, for everyone; in your love a measure for all that is to be. Not in the sense that the rest of the world seems obscure tome, on the contrary, your love makes it clear; I see quite clearly what men are like and what they plan, wish, do and enjoy; I don't grudge them what they have, and comparing is a secret joy to me, possessing as I do such an imperishable treasure.

You in your household must feel as I often do in my affairs; we often don't notice objects simply because we don't choose to look at them, but things acquire an interest as soon as we see clearly the way they are related to each other. For we always like to join in, and the good man takes pleasure in arranging, putting in order and furthering the right and its peaceful rule. Adieu, you whom I love a thousand times.

Victor Hugo

To Adele Foucher

My dearest,

When two souls, which have sought each other for, however long in the throng, have finally found each other ...a union, fiery and pure as they themselves are... begins on earth and continues forever in heaven.

This union is love, true love, ... a religion, which deifies the loved one, whose life comes from devotion and passion, and for which the greatest sacrifices are the sweetest delights.

This is the love which you inspire in me... Your soul is made to love with the purity and passion of angels; but perhaps it can only love another angel, in which case I must tremble with apprehension.

Yours forever,
Victor Hugo (1821)

Victor Hugo

Friday evening, March 15, 1822,

After the two delightful evenings spent yesterday and the day before, I shall certainly not go out tonight, but will sit here at home and write to you. Besides, my Adele, my adorable and adored Adele, what have I not to tell you? O, God! for two days, I have been asking myself every moment if such happiness is not a dream. It seems to me that what I feel is not of earth. I cannot yet comprehend this cloudless heaven.

You do not yet know, Adele, to what I had resigned myself. Alas, do I know it myself? Because I was weak, I fancied I was calm; because I was preparing myself for all the mad follies of despair, I thought I was courageous and resigned. Ah! let me cast myself humbly at your feet, you who are so grand, so tender and strong! I had been thinking that the utmost limit of my devotion could only be the sacrifice of my life; but you, my generous love, were ready to sacrifice for me the repose of yours.

...You have been privileged to receive every gift from nature, you have both fortitude and tears. Oh, Adele, do not mistake these words for blind enthusiasm - enthusiasm for you has lasted all my life, and increased day by day. My whole soul is yours. If my entire existence had not been yours, the harmony of my being would have been lost, and I must have died -- died inevitably.

These were my meditations, Adele, when the letter that was to bring me hope of else despair arrived. If you love me, you know what must have been my joy. What I know you may have felt, I will not describe.

My Adele, why is there no word for this but joy? Is it because there is no power in human speech to express such happiness?

The sudden bound from mournful resignation to infinite felicity seemed to upset me. Even now I am still beside myself and sometimes I tremble lest I should suddenly awaken from this dream divine.

Oh, now you are mine! At last you are mine! Soon -- in a few months, perhaps, my angel will sleep in my arms, will awaken in my arms, will live there. All your thoughts at all moments, all your looks will be for me; all my thoughts, all my moments, all my looks, will be for you! My Adele!

Adieu, my angel, my beloved Adele! Adieu! I will kiss your hair and go to bed. Still I am far from you, but I can dream of you. Soon perhaps you will be at my side. Adieu; pardon the delirium of your husband who embraces you, and who adores you, both for this life and another.

Victor Hugo

December 31st, 1851

You have been wonderful, my Juliette, all through these dark and violent days. If I needed love, you brought it to me, bless you! When, in my hiding places, always dangerous, after a night of waiting, I heard the key of my door trembling in your fingers, peril and darkness were no longer round me--what entered then was light!

We must never forget those terrible, but so sweet, hours when you were close to me in the intervals of fighting. Let us remember all our lives that dark little room, the ancient hangings, the two armchairs, side by side, the meal we ate off the corner of the table, the cold chicken you had brought; our sweet converse, your caresses, your anxieties, your devotion. You were surprised to find me calm and serene. Do you know whence came both calmness and serenity? From you...

To Peter Abelard

To Peter

To her only one after Christ, she who is his alone in Christ.

...We were greatly surprised when instead of bringing us the healing balm of comfort you increased our desolation and made the tears to flow which you should have dried. For which of us could remain dry-eyed on hearing the words you wrote towards the end of your letter: 'But if the Lord shall deliver me into the hands of my enemies so that they overcome and kill me...'? My dearest, how could you think such a thought? How could you give voice to it? Never may God be so forgetful of his humble handmaids as to let them outlive you; never may he grant us a life which would be harder to bear than any form of death.

The proper course would be for you to perform our funeral rites, for you to commend our souls to God, and to send ahead of you those whom you assembled for God's service -- so that you need no longer be troubled by worries for us, and follow after us the more gladly because freed from concern for our salvation.

Spare us, I implore you, master, spare us words such as these which can only intensify our existing unhappiness; do not deny us, before death, the one thing by which we live. 'Each day has trouble enough of its own,' and the day, shrouded in bitterness, will bring with it distress enough to all it comes upon. 'Why is it necessary,' says Seneca, 'to summon evil' and to destroy life before death comes?

You ask us, my love, if you chance to die when absent from us, to have your body brought to our burial-ground so that you may reap a fuller harvest from the prayers we shall offer in constant memory of you. But how could you suppose that our memory of you could ever fade? Besides, what time will there be then which will be fitting for prayer, when extreme distress will allow us no peace, when the soul will lose its power of reason and the tongue its use of speech? Or when the frantic mind, far from being resigned, may even (if I may so) rage against God himself, and provoke him with complaints instead of placating him with prayers?

In our misery then we shall have time only for tears and no power to pray; we shall be hurrying to follow, not to bury you, so that we may share your grave instead of laying you in it. If we lose our life in you, we shall not be able to go on living when you leave us.

I would not even have us live to see that day, for if the mere mention of your death is death for us, what will the reality be if it finds us still alive? God grant we may never live on to perform this duty, to render you the service which we look for from you alone; in this may we go before, not after you!

Heloise

To Peter Abelard

To Peter Abelard:

I have your picture in my room. I never pass by it without stopping to look at it; and yet when you were present with me, I scare ever cast my eyes upon it. If a picture which is but a mute representation of an object can give such pleasure, what cannot letters inspire? They have souls, they can speak, they have in them all that force which expresses the transport of the heart; they have all the fire of our passions....

Heloise

Lyman Hodge

February 10, 1867

...and now, love, you with the warm heart and loving eyes, whose picture I kissed last night and whose lips I so often kiss in my dreams, whose love enriches me so bountifully with all pleasant memories and sweet anticipations, whose encircling arms shield me from so much evil and harm, whose caresses are so dear and so longed for awake and in slumber, making my heart beat faster, my flesh tremble and my brain giddy with delight, - whose feet I kiss and whose knees I embrace as a devotee kisses and embraces those of his idol, - my darling whose home is in my arms and whose resting place my bosom, who first came to them as a frightened bird but now loves to linger there till long after the midnight chimes have uttered their warning, - my life, with your generous soul, my heart's keeper and my true lover, - Good night: a good night and a fair one to thy sleeping eyes and wearied limb, the precursor of many bright, beautiful mornings when my kisses shall waken thee and my love shall greet thee.

Lyman

Count Gabriel Honore de Mirbeau

Circa 1780

Sophie,

To be with the people one loves, says La Bruyere is enough -- to dream you are speaking to them, not speaking to them, thinking of them, thinking of the most indifferent things, but by their side, nothing else matters. O mon amie, how true that is! and it is also true that when one acquires such a habit, it becomes a necessary part of one's existence.

Alas! I well know, I should know too well, since the three months that I sigh, far away from thee, that I possess thee no more, than my happiness has departed. However, when every morning I wake up, I look for you, it seems to me that half of myself is missing, and that is too true.

Twenty times during the day, I ask myself where you are; judge how strong the illusion is, and how cruel it is to see it vanish. When I go to bed, I do not fail to make room for you; I push myself quite close to the wall and leave a great empty space in my small bed. This movement is mechanical, these thoughts are involuntary. Ah! how one accustoms oneself to happiness.

Alas! one only knows it well when one has lost it, and I'm sure we have only learnt to appreciate how necessary we are to each other, since the thunderbolt has parted us. The source of our tears has not dried up, dear Sophie; we cannot become healed; we have enough in our hearts to love always, and, because of that, enough to weep always.

Gabriel

James Joyce

15 August, 1904

My dear Nora,

It has just struck me. I came in at half past eleven. Since then I have been sitting in an easy chair like a fool. I could do nothing. I hear nothing but your voice. I am like a fool hearing you call me 'Dear.' I offended two men today by leaving them coolly. I wanted to hear your voice, not theirs.

When I am with you I leave aside my contemptuous, suspicious nature. I wish I felt your head on my shoulder. I think I will go to bed.

I have been a half-hour writing this thing. Will you write something to me? I hope you will. How am I to sign myself? I won't sign anything at all, because I don't know what to sign myself.

John Keats

March 1820

Sweetest Fanny,

You fear, sometimes, I do not love you so much as you wish? My dear Girl I love you ever and ever and without reserve. The more I have known you the more have I lov'd. In every way - even my jealousies have been agonies of Love, in the hottest fit I ever had I would have died for you. I have vex'd you too much. But for Love! Can I help it? You are always new. The last of your kisses was ever the sweetest; the last smile the brightest; the last movement the gracefullest. When you pass'd my window home yesterday, I was fill'd with as much admiration as if I had then seen you for the first time. You uttered a half complaint once that I only lov'd your Beauty. Have I nothing else then to love in you but that? Do not I see a heart naturally furnish'd with wings imprison itself with me? No ill prospect has been able to turn your thoughts a moment from me. This perhaps should be as much a subject of sorrow as joy - but I will not talk of that. Even if you did not love me I could not help an entire devotion to you: how much more deeply then must I feel for you knowing you love me. My Mind has been the most discontented and restless one that ever was put into a body too small for it. I never felt my Mind repose upon anything with complete and undistracted enjoyment - upon no person but you. When you are in the room my thoughts never fly out of window: you always concentrate my whole senses. The anxiety shown about our Love in your last note is an immense pleasure to me; however you must not suffer such speculations to molest you any more: not will I any more believe you can have the least pique against me. Brown is gone out - - but here is Mrs Wylie -- when she is gone I shall be awake for you. -- Remembrances to your Mother.

Your affectionate, J. Keats

John Keats

To Fanny Brawne:

I cannot exist without you - I am forgetful of every thing but seeing you again - my life seems to stop there - I see no further. You have absorb'd me.

I have a sensation at the present moment as though I were dissolving ....I have been astonished that men could die martyrs for religion - I have shudder'd at it - I shudder no more - I could be martyr'd for my religion - love is my religion - I could die for that - I could die for you. My creed is love and you are its only tenet - you have ravish'd me away by a power I cannot resist.

- John Keats

John Keats

Wednesday Morng. [Kentish Town, 1820]

My Dearest Girl,

I have been a walk this morning with a book in my hand, but as usual I have been occupied with nothing but you: I wish I could say in an agreeable manner. I am tormented day and night. They talk of my going to Italy. 'Tis certain I shall never recover if I am to be so long separate from you: yet with all this devotion to you I cannot persuade myself into any confidence of you....

You are to me an object intensely desirable -- the air I breathe in a room empty of you in unhealthy. I am not the same to you -- no -- you can wait -- you have a thousand activities -- you can be happy without me. Any party, anything to fill up the day has been enough.

How have you pass'd this month? Who have you smil'd with? All this may seem savage in me. You do no feel as I do -- you do not know what it is to love -- one day you may -- your time is not come....

I cannot live without you, and not only you but chaste you; virtuous you. The Sun rises and sets, the day passes, and you follow the bent of your inclination to a certain extent -- you have no conception of the quantity of miserable feeling that passes through me in a day -- Be serious! Love is not a plaything -- and again do not write unless you can do it with a crystal conscience. I would sooner die for want of you than ---

Yours for ever

J. Keats

Franz Kafka

11 November, 1912

Fräulein Felice!

I am now going to ask you a favor which sounds quite crazy, and which I should regard as such, were I the one to receive the letter. It is also the very greatest test that even the kindest person could be put to. Well, this is it:

Write to me only once a week, so that your letter arrives on Sunday - - for I cannot endure your daily letters, I am incapable of enduring them. For instance, I answer one of your letters, then lie in bed in apparent calm, but my heart beats through my entire body and is conscious only of you. I belong to you; there is really no other way of expressing it, and that is not strong enough. But for this very reason I don't want to know what you are wearing; it confuses me so much that I cannot deal with life; and that's why I don't want to know that you are fond of me. If I did, how could I, fool that I am, go on sitting in my office, or here at home, instead of leaping onto a train with my eyes shut and opening them only when I am with you? Oh, there is a sad, sad reason for not doing so. To make it short: My health is only just good enough for myself alone, not good enough for marriage, let alone fatherhood. Yet when I read your letter, I feel I could overlook even what cannot possibly be overlooked.

If only I had your answer now! And how horribly I torment you, and how I compel you, in the stillness of your room, to read this letter, as nasty a letter as has ever lain on your desk! Honestly, it strikes me sometimes that I prey like a spectre on your felicitous name! If only I had mailed Saturday's letter, in which I implored you never to write to me again, and in which I gave a similar promise. Oh God, what prevented me from sending that letter? All would be well. But is a peaceful solution possible now? Would it help if we wrote to each other only once a week? No, if my suffering could be cured by such means it would not be serious. And already I foresee that I shan't be able to endure even the Sunday letters. And so, to compensate for Saturday's lost opportunity, I ask you with what energy remains to me at the end of this letter: If we value our lives, let us abandon it all.

Did I think of signing myself Dein? No, nothing could be more false. No, I am forever fettered to myself, that's what I am, and that's what I must try to live with.

Franz

Fanny Kemble

London, December 1842 or early 1843

Having loved you well enough to give you my life when it was best work giving --having made you the center of all my hopes of earthly happiness -- having never loved any human being as I have loved you, you can never be to me like any other human being, and it is utterly impossible that I should ever regard you with indifference.

My whole existence having once had you for its sole object, and all its thoughts, hopes, affections having, in their full harvest, been yours, it is utterly impossible that I should ever forget this--that I should ever forget that you were once my lover and are my husband and the father of my children. I cannot behold you without emotion; my heart still answers to your voice, my blood in my veins to your footsteps.

King Henry IV of France

June 16, 1593

I have waited patiently for one whole day without news of you; I have been counting the time and that's what it must be. But a second day--I can see no reason for it, unless my servants have grown lazy or been captured by the enemy, for I dare not put the blame on you, my beautiful angel: I am too confident of your affection--which is certainly due to me, for my love was never greater, nor my desire more urgent; that is why I repeat this refrain in all my letters: come, come, come, my dear love.

Honor with your presence the man who, if only he were free, would go a thousand miles to throw himself at your feet and never move from there. As for what is happening here, we have drained the water from the moat, but our cannons are not going to be in place until Friday when, God willing, I will dine in town.

The day after you reach Mantes, my sister will arrive at Anet, where I will have the pleasure of seeing you every day. I am sending you a bouquet of orange blossom that I have just received. I kiss the hands of the Vicomtess [Gabrielle's sister, Fran oise] if she is there, and of my good friend [his sister, Catherine of Bourbon], and as for you, my dear love, I kiss your feet a million times.

King Henry VIII of England

To Anne Boleyn

My Mistress and Friend,

I and my heart put ourselves in your hands, begging you to recommend us to your good grace and not to let absence lessen your affection...or myself the pang of absence is already to great, and when I think of the increase of what I must needs suffer it would be well nigh intolerable but for my firm hope of your unchangeable affection...

Henry VIII (1528)

King Henry VIII of England

Circa1528

In debating with myself the contents of your letters I have been put to a great agony; not knowing how to understand them, whether to my disadvantage as shown in some places, or to my advantage as in others. I beseech you now with all my heart definitely to let me know your whole mind as to the love between us; for necessity compels me to plague you for a reply, having been for more than a year now struck by the dart of love, and being uncertain either of failure or of finding a place in your heart and affection, which point has certainly kept me for some time from naming you my mistress, since if you only love me with an ordinary love the name is not appropriate to you, seeing that it stands for an uncommon position very remote from the ordinary; but if it pleases you to do the duty of a true, loyal mistress and friend, and to give yourself body and heart to me, who have been, and will be, your very loyal servant (if your rigour does not forbid me), I promise you that not only the name will be due to you, but also to take you as my sole mistress, casting off all others than yourself out of mind and affection, and to serve you only; begging you to make me a complete reply to this my rude letter as to how far and in what I can trust; and if it does not please you to reply in writing, to let me know of some place where I can have it by word of mouth, the which place I will seek out with all my heart. No more for fear of wearying you. Written by the hand of him who would willingly remain yours.

HR

Julia Lee Booker

July 24, 1940

I cannot get that beautiful afternoon out of my head, above me where I lay the grass was silhouetted against the blue of the heavens, small clouds were rushing past as the wind drove them on an endless journey. Then close to me was the most lovely of all, your soft hair against my cheek, your kisses so cool and unearthly and my happiness was so great.

Katherine Mansfield

Saturday Night, May 19, 1917

My darling,

Do not imagine, because you find these lines in your journal that I have been trespassing. You know I have not - and where else shall I leave a love letter? For I long to write you a love-letter tonight.

You are all about me - I seem to breathe you, hear you, feel you in me and of me.

What am I doing here? You are away. I have seen you in the train, at the station, driving up, sitting in the lamplight, talking, greeting people, washing your hands... And I am here - in your tent - sitting at your table.

There are some wall-flower petals on the table and a dead match, a blue pencil and a Magdeburgische Zeitung. I am just as much at home as they.

When dusk came, flowing up the silent garden, lapping against the blind windows, my first and last terror started up. I was making some coffee in the kitchen. It was so violent, so dreadful I put down the coffee pot - and simply ran away - ran ran out of the studio and up the street with my bag under one arm and a block of writing paper and a pen under the other. I felt that if I could get here and find Mrs. F I should be *safe*.

I found her and I lighted your gas, wound up your clock, drew your curtains and embraced your black overcoat before I sat down, frightened no longer. Do not be angry with me, Bogey. Ca a ete plus fort que moi .... That is why I am here.

When you came to tea this afternoon you took a brioche, broke it in half and padded the inside doughy bit with two fingers. You always do that with a bun or roll or a piece of bread. It is your way - your head a little on one side the while.

When you opened your suitcase, I saw your old Feltie and a French book and a com all higgledy-piggledy. 'Tig, Ive only got 3 handkerchiefs.' Why should that memory be so sweet to me?...

Last night, there was a moment before you got into bed. You stood, quite naked, bending forward a little, talking. It was only for an instant. I saw you - I loved you so, loved your body with such tenderness. Ah, my dear!

And I am not thinking of *passion*. No, of that other thing that makes me feel that every inch of you is so precious to me - your soft shoulders - your creamy warm skin, your ears cold like shells are cold - your long legs and your feet that I love to clasp with my feet - the feeling of your belly - and your thin young back. Just below that bone that sticks out at the back of your neck you have a little mole.

It is partly because we are young that I feel this tenderness. I love your mouth. I could not bear that it should be touched even by a cold wind if I were the Lord.

We two, you know, have everything before us, and we shall do very great things. I have perfect faith in us, and so perfect is my love for you that I am, as it were, still, silent to my very soul.

I want nobody but you for my lover and my friend and to nobody buy you shall I be faithful.

I am yours forever.

Tig.

Katherine Mansfield

January 27, 1918

My love for you tonight is so deep and tender that it seems to be outside myself as well. I am fast shut up like a little lake in the embrace of some big mountains. If you were to climb up the mountains, you would see me down below, deep and shining - and quite fathomless, my dear. You might drop your heart into me and you'd never hear it touch bottom.

I love you - I love you - Goodnight. Oh Bogey, what it is to love like this!

Jack London

Oakland, April 3, 1901

Dear Anna:

Did I say that the human might be filed in categories? Well, and if I did, let me qualify -- not all humans. You elude me. I cannot place you, cannot grasp you. I may boast that of nine out of ten, under given circumstances, I can forecast their action; that of nine out of ten, by their word or action, I may feel the pulse of their hearts. But of the tenth I despair. It is beyond me. You are that tenth.

Were ever two souls, with dumb lips, more incongruously matched! We may feel in common -- surely, we oftimes do -- and when we do not feel in common, yet do we understand; and yet we have no common tongue. Spoken words do not come to us. We are unintelligible. God must laugh at the mummery.

The one gleam of sanity through it all is that we are both large temperamentally, large enough to often understand. True, we often understand but in vague glimmering ways, by dim perceptions, like ghosts, which, while we doubt, haunt us with their truth. And still, I, for one, dare not believe; for you are that tenth which I may not forecast.

Am I unintelligible now? I do not know. I imagine so. I cannot find the common tongue.

Large temperamentally -- that is it. It is the one thing that brings us at all in touch. We have, flashed through us, you and I, each a bit of universal, and so we draw together. And yet we are so different.

I smile at you when you grow enthusiastic? It is a forgivable smile -- nay, almost an envious smile. I have lived twenty-five years of repression. I learned not to be enthusiastic. It is a hard lesson to forget. I begin to forget, but it is so little. At the best, before I die, I cannot hope to forget all or most. I can exult, now that I am learning, in little things, in other things; but of my things, and secret things doubly mine, I cannot, I cannot. Do I make myself intelligible? Do you hear my voice? I fear not. There are poseurs. I am the most successful of them all.

Jack

Franz Liszt

Thursday morning 1834

My heart overflows with emotion and joy! I do not know what heavenly languor, what infinite pleasure permeates it and burns me up. It is as if I had never loved!!! Tell me whence these uncanny disturbances spring, these inexpressible foretastes of delight, these divine, tremors of love. Oh! all this can only spring from you, sister, angel, woman, Marie! All this can only be, is surely nothing less than a gentle ray streaming from your fiery soul, or else some secret poignant teardrop which you have long since left in my breast.

My God, my God, never force us apart, take pity on us! But what am I saying? Forgive my weakness, how couldst Thou divide us! Thou wouldst have nothing but pity for us...No no! It is not in vain that our flesh and our souls quicken and become immortal through Thy Word, which cries out deep within us Father, Father...out Thy hand to us, that our broken hearts seek their refuge in Thee...O! we thank, bless and praise Thee, O God, for all that Thou has given us, and all that Thou hast prepared for us....

This is to be -- to be!

Marie! Marie!

Oh let me repeat that name a hundred times, a thousand times over; for three days now it has lived within me, oppressed me, set me afire. I am not writing to you, no, I am close beside you. I see you, I hear you. Eternity in your arms... Heaven, Hell, everything, all is within you, redoubled... Oh! Leave me free to rave in my delirium. Drab, tame, constricting reality is no longer enough for me. We must live our lives to the full, loving and suffering to extremes!...

Franz

Franz Liszt

December 1834

Marie! Marie!

Oh let me repeat that name a hundred times,
a thousand times over;
for three days now it has lived within me, oppressed me,
set me afire.
I am not writing to you, no, I am close beside you.
I see you,
I hear you...
Eternity in your arms...Heaven, hell,
all is within you and even more than all...
Oh! Leave me free to rave in my delirium.
Mean, cautious, narrow reality is no longer enough for me.
We must live out lives to the full,
our loves, our sorrow...!
Oh! you believe me capable of
self-sacrifice, chastity, temperance
and piety, do you not?
But let no more be said of this...
it is for you to question, to draw conclusions,
to save me as you see fit.
Let me be mad, senseless
since you can do nothing, nothing
at all for me.
It is good for me to speak to you now.
This is to be! To be!!!

Laura Mary Octavia Lyttleton

February   1886

My will made by me, Laura Mary Octavia Lyttleton.

I have not much to leave behind me, should I die next month, having my treasure deep in my heart where no one can reach it, and where even death cannot enter...

I want, first of all, to tell Alfred that all I have in the world and all I am and ever shall be, belongs to him more than anyone...

So few women have been as happy as I have been every hour since I married - so few have had such a wonderful sky of love for their common atmosphere, that perhaps it will seem strange when I write down that the sadness of death and parting is greatly lessened to me by the fact of my consciousness of the eternal, indivisible oneness of Alfred and me.

I feel as long as he is down here I must be here, silently, secretly sitting beside him as I do every evening now, however much my soul is the other side, and that if Alfred were to die, we would be as we were on earth, love as we did this year, only fuller, quicker, deeper than ever, with a purer passion and a wiser worship.

Only in the meantime, whilst my body is hid from him and my eyes cannot see him, let my trivial toys be his till the morning comes when nothing will matter because all is spirit.

Thomas Otway

Could I see you without passion, or be absent from you without pain, I need not beg your pardon for thus renewing my vows that I love you more than health, or any happiness here or hereafter.

Everything you do is a new charm to me, and though I have languished for seven long tedious years of desire, jealously despairing, yet every minute I see you I still discover something new and more bewitching. Consider how I love you; what would I not renounce or enterprise for you?

I much have you mine, or I am miserable, and nothing but knowing which shall be the happy hour can make the rest of my years that are to come tolerable. Give me a word or two of comfort, or resolve never to look on me more, for I cannot bear a kind look and after it a cruel denial.

This minute my heart aches for you; and, if I cannot have a right in yours, I wish it would ache till I could complain to you no longer.

Publius Ovidius Naso

Circa A.D. 8-17

I plowed the vast ocean on a frail bit of timber; (whereas) the ship that bore the son of AEson (Jason) was strong... The furtive arts of Cupid aided him; arts which I wish that Love had not learned from me. He returned home; I shall die in these lands, if the heavy wrath of the offended God shall be lasting.

My burden, most faithful wife, is a harder one than that which the son of AEson bore. You, too, whom I left still young at my departure from the City, I can believe to have grown old under my calamities. Oh, grant it, ye Gods, that I may be enabled to see you, even if such, and to give the joyous kiss on each cheek in its turn; and to embrace your emaciated body in my arms, and to say, "'twas anxiety, on my account, that caused this thinness"; and, weeping, to recount in person my sorrows to you in tears, and thus enjoy a conversation that I had never hoped for; and to offer the due frankincense, with grateful hand, to the Caesars, and to the wife that is worthy of a Caesar, Deities in real truth!

Oh, that the mother of Menon, that Prince being softened, would with her rosy lips, speedily call forth that day.

Robert Peary

August 17, 1908

S.S. Roosevelt,

My Darling Josephine: Am nearly through with my writing. Am brain weary with the thousand and one imperative details and things to think of. Everything thus far has gone well, too well I am afraid, and I am (solely on general principles) somewhat suspicious of the future. The ship is in better shape than before; the party and crew are apparently harmonious; I have 21 Eskimo men (against 23 last time) but the total of men women and children is only 50 as against 67 before owing to a more careful selection as to children... I have landed supplies here, and leave two men ostensibly on behalf of Cook.

As a matter of fact I have established here the sub-base which last I established at Victoria Head, as a precaution in event of loss of the Roosevelt either going up this fall or coming down next summer. In some respects this is an advantage as on leaving here there is nothing to delay me or keep me from taking either side of the Channel going up. the conditions give me entire control of the situation...

You have been with me constantly, sweetheart. At Kangerdlooksoah I looked repeatedly at Ptarmigan Island and thought of the time we camped there. At Nuuatoksoah I landed where we were. And on the 11th we passed the mouth of Bowdoin Bay in brilliant weather, and as long as I could I kept my eyes on Anniversary Lodge. We have been great chums dear. Tell Marie to remember what I told her, tell "Mister Man" [Robert Peary, Jr.] to remember "straight and strong and clean and honest", obey orders, and never forget that Daddy put "Mut" in his charge till he himself comes back to take her. In fancy I kiss your dear eyes and lips and cheeks sweetheart; and dream of you and my children, and my home till I come again. Kiss my babies for me. Aufwiedersehen.

Love, Love, Love. Your Bert

P.S. August 18, 9 a.m. ...Tell Marie that her fir pillow perfumes me to sleep.

Sir Walter Raleigh

1603

You shall now receive (my dear wife) my last words in these my last lines. My love I send you that you may keep it when I am dead, and my counsel that you may remember it when I am no more.

I would not by my will present you with sorrows (dear Besse) let them go to the grave with me and be buried in the dust. And seeing that it is not God's will that I should see you any more in this life, bear it patiently, and with a heart like thy self.

First, I send you all the thanks which my heart can conceive, or my words can rehearse for your many travails, and care taken for me, which though they have not taken effect as you wished, yet my debt to you is not the less; but pay it I never shall in this world.

Secondly, I beseech you for the love you bear me living, do not hide your self many days, but by your travails seek to help your miserable fortunes and the right of your poor child. Thy mourning cannot avail me, I am but dust...

Remember your poor child for his father's sake, who chose you, and loved you in his happiest times. Get those letters which I wrote to the Lords, wherein I sued for my life; God is my witness it was for you and yours that I desired life, but it is true that I disdained my self for begging of it: for know it that your son is the son of a true man, and one who in his own respect despiseth death and all his misshapen and ugly forms.

I cannot write much, God he knows how hardly I steal this time while others sleep, and it is also time that I should separate my thoughts from the world. Beg my dead body which living was denied thee; and either lay it at Sherburne or in Exeter Church, by my Father and Mother; I can say no more, time and death call me away....

Written with the dying hand of sometimes they Husband, but now alas overthrown. Yours that was, but now not my own.

Walter Raleigh

John Ruskin

December 1847

I don't know anything dreadful enough to liken to you - you are like a sweet forest of pleasant glades and whispering branches - where people wander on and on in its playing shadows they know not how far - and when they come near the centre of it, it is all cold and impenetrable - and when they would fain turn, lo - they are hedged with briars and thorns and cannot escape...

You are like the bright - soft - swelling - lovely fields of a high glacier covered with fresh morning snow - which is heavenly to the eye - and soft and winning on the foot - but beneath, there are winding clefts and dark places in its cold - cold ice - where men fall, and rise not again.

Robert Schumann

1838

Clara,

How happy your last letters have made me -- those since Christmas Eve! I should like to call you by all the endearing epithets, and yet I can find no lovelier word than the simple word 'dear,' but there is a particular way of saying it. My dear one, then, I have wept for joy to think that you are mine, and often wonder if I deserve you.

One would think that no one man's heart and brain could stand all the things that are crowded into one day. Where do these thousands of thoughts, wishes, sorrows, joys and hopes come from? Day in, day out, the procession goes on. But how light-hearted I was yesterday and the day before! There shone out of your letters so noble a spirit, such faith, such a wealth of love!

What would I not do for love of you, my own Clara! The knights of old were better off; they could go through fire or slay dragons to win their ladies, but we of today have to content ourselves with more prosaic methods, such as smoking fewer cigars, and the like. After all, though, we can love, knights or no knights; and so, as ever, only the times change, not men's hearts...

You cannot think how your letter has raised and strengthened me... You are splendid, and I have much more reason to be proud of you than you of me. I have made up my mind, though, to read all your wishes in your face. Then you will think, even though you don't say it, that your Robert is a really good sort, that he is entirely yours, and he loves you more than words can say.

You shall indeed have cause to think so in the happy future. I still see you as you looked in your little cap that last evening. I still hear you call me du. Clara, I heard nothing of what you said but that du. Don't you remember?

But I see you in many another unforgettable guise. Once you were in a black dress, going to the theatre with Emilia List; it was during our separation. I know you will not have forgotten; it is vivid with me. Another time you were walking in the Thomasgasschen with an umbrella up, and you avoided me in desperation. And yet another time, as you were putting on your hat after a concert, our eyes happened to meet, and yours were full of the old unchanging love.

I picture you in all sorts of ways, as I have seen you since. I did not look at you much, but you charmed me so immeasurably... Ah, I can never praise you enough for yourself or for your love of me, which I don't really deserve.

Robert

Lady Shigenari To Lord Shigenari

16th Century

I know that when two wayfarers 'take shelter under the same tree and slake their thirst in the same river' it has all been determined by their karma from a previous life. For the past few years you and I have shared the same pillow as man and wife who had intended to live and grow old together, and I have become as attached to you as your own shadow. This is what I believed, and I think this is what you have also thought about us.

But now I have learnt about the final enterprise on which you have decided and, though I cannot be with you to share the grand moment, I rejoice in the knowledge of it. It is said that (on the eve of his final battle) the Chinese general, Hsiang Yü, valiant warrior though he was, grieved deeply about leaving Lady Yü, and that (in our own country) Kiso Yoshinaka lamented his parting from Lady Matsudono. I have now abandoned all hope about our future together in this world, and (mindful of their example) I have resolved to take the ultimate step while you are still alive. I shall be waiting for you at the end of what they call the road to death.

I pray that you may never, never forget the great bounty, deep as the ocean, high as the mountains, that has been bestowed upon us for so many years by our lord, Prince Hideyori.

Sir Richard Steele

1707
Smith-street
West-minster

Madam,

I lay down last night with your image in my thoughts, and have awak'd this morning in the same contemplation. The pleasing transport ith which I'm delighted, has a sweetnesse in it attended with a train of ten thousand soft desires, anxieties, and cares.

The day arises on my hopes with new brightnesse; youth beauty and innocence are the charming objects that steal me from myself, and give me joys above the reach of ambition pride or glory. Believe me, Fair One, to throw myself at yr feet is giving myself the highest blisse I know of earth.

Oh hasten ye minutes! Bring on the happy morning wherein to be ever her's will make me look down on Thrones!

Dear Molly I am tenderly, passionately, faithfully thine,

Richard Steele

Leo Tolstoy

November 2, 1856

I already love in you your beauty, but I am only beginning to love in you that which is eternal and ever precious - your heart, your soul. Beauty one could get to know and fall in love with in one hour and cease to love it as speedily; but the soul one must learn to know. Believe me, nothing on earth is given without labour, even love, the most beautiful and natural of feelings.

Tsarina Alexandra to Tsar Nicholas II

December 30, 1915

Off you go again alone and its with a very heavy heart I part from you. No more kisses and tender caresses for ever so long -- I want to bury myself in you, hold you tight in my arms, make you feel the intense love of mine.

You are my very life Sweetheart, and every separation gives such endless heartache...

Goodbye my Angel, Husband of my heart I envy my flowers that will accompany you. I press you tightly to my breast, kiss every sweet place with tender love...

God bless and protect you, guard you from all harm, guide you safely and firmly into the new year. May it bring glory and sure peace, and the reward for all this war has cost you.

I gently press my lips to yours and try to forget everything, gazing into your lovely eyes - I lay on your precious breast, rested my tired head upon it still. This morning I tried to gain calm and strength for the separation. Goodbye wee one, Lovebird, Sunshine, Huzy mine, Own!

Henry Von Kleist

1810

My golden child, my pearl, my precious stone, my crown, my queen and empress. You dear darling of my heart, my highest and most precious, my all and everything, my wife, the baptism of my children, my tragic play, my posthumous reputation. Ach! You are my second better self, my virtues, my merits, my hope, the forgiveness of my sins, my future sanctity, O little daughter of heaven, my child of God, my intercessor, my guardian angel, my cherubim and seraph, how I love you!

To Thomas Carlyle

October 3, 1826

...it is so easy a thing for you to lift me to Seventh Heaven! My soul was darker than midnight, when your pen said "let there be light." and there was light as at the bidding of the Word... When I read in your looks and words that you love me, I feel it in the deepest part of my soul; and then I care not one straw for the whole Universe beside...

Edith Wharton

There would have been the making of an accomplished flirt in me, because my lucidity shows me each move of the game - but that, in the same instant, a reaction of contempt makes me sweep all the counters off the board and cry out: - "Take them all - I don't want to win - I want to lose everything to you!"

Mary Wollstonecraft

October 4, 1796

I would have liked to have dined with you today, after finishing your essay - that my eyes, and lips, I do not exactly mean my voice, might have told you that they had raised you in my esteem. What a cold word! I would say love, if you will promise not to dispute about its propriety, when I want to express an increasing affection, founded on a more intimate acquaintance with your heart and understanding.

I shall cork up all my kindness - yet the fine volatile essence may fly off in my walk - you know not how much tenderness for you may escape in a voluptuous sigh, should the air, as is often the case, give a pleasurable movement to the sensations, that have been clustering round my heart, as I read this morning - reminding myself, every now and then, that the writer loved me.

Voluptuous is often expressive of a meaning I do not now intend to give, I would describe one of those moments, when the senses are exactly tuned by the ringing tenderness of the heart and according reason entices you to live in the present moment, regardless of the past or future - it is not rapture - it is sublime tranquility.

I have felt it in your arms - hush! Let not the light see, I was going to say hear it - these confessions should only be uttered - you know where, when the curtains are up - and all the world shut out - Ah me!

I wish I may find you at home when I carry this letter to drop it in the box, - that I may drop a kiss with it into your heart, to be embalmed, till me meet, closer.

Mary Wordsworth to William Wordsworth

August 1, 1810

Oh My William! it is not in my power to tell thee how I have been affected by this dearest of all letters - it was so unexpected - so new a thing to see the breathing of thy inmost heart upon paper that I was quite overpowered, & now that I sit down to answer thee in the loneliness & depth of that love which unites us & which cannot be felt but by ourselves, I am so agitated & my eyes are so bedimmed that I scarcely know how to proceed...

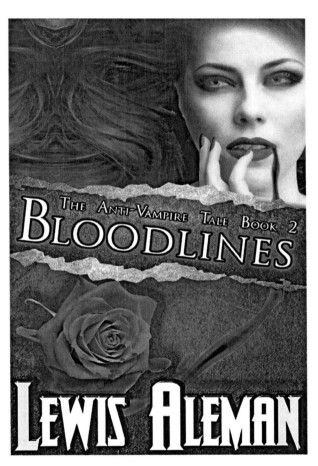

CPSIA information can be obtained at www.ICGtesting.com
Printed in the USA
BVOW03s0754201214

380000BV00010B/189/P